743
Ame

Ames, Lee J.
Draw 50 athletes

Draw
50
Athletes

BOOKS IN THIS SERIES

Draw 50 Athletes

Lee J. Ames

MAIN
STREET
BOOKS

Doubleday
New York London Toronto Sydney Auckland

A MAIN STREET BOOK
PUBLISHED BY DOUBLEDAY
a division of Bantam Doubleday Dell Publishing Group, Inc.
1540 Broadway, New York, New York 10036

MAIN STREET BOOKS, DOUBLEDAY, and the portrayal of a
building with a tree are trademarks of Doubleday, a
division of Bantam Doubleday Dell Publishing Group, Inc.

Library of Congress Cataloging-in-Publication Data
Ames, Lee J.
    Draw 50 athletes.
    Summary: Step-by-step instructions on how to draw a
variety of athletes from a number of action perspectives.
    1. Action in art—Juvenile literature.   2. Athletes
in art—Juvenile literature.   3. Wrestlers in art—
Juvenile literature.   4. Drawing—Techniques—Juvenile
literature.   [1. Athletes in art.   2. Drawing—Technique]
I. Title.   II. Title: Draw fifty athletes.
NC785.A46   1985   743'.4   83.45569
ISBN 0-385-19055-7
ISBN 0-385-19056-5 (lib. bdg.)
ISBN 0-385-24638-2 (pbk)

To Jonathan and Cindy,
my favorite athletes,
with much love . . .

. . . and thanks to Warren Budd for all his help.

To the Reader

This book of 50 athletes will show you a method of drawing the human figure, of searching out the basic simple forms and lightly building one on the other. When these forms add up to a complete figure, drawn very lightly up to this point, the drawing is finished with firm, dark lines.

You need not start with the first illustration. Choose whichever you wish. When you have decided, follow the step-by-step method shown. *Very lightly* and *carefully*, sketch out step number one. However, this step, which is the easiest, should be done *most carefully*. Step number two is added right to step number one, also lightly and also very carefully. Step number 3 is sketched right on top of numbers one and two. Continue this way to the last step.

It may seem strange to ask you to be extra careful when you are drawing what seem to be the easiest first steps, but this is most important, for a careless mistake at the beginning may spoil the whole picture at the end. As you sketch out each step, watch the spaces between the lines, as well as the lines, and see that they are the same. After each step, you may want to lighten your work by pressing it with a kneaded eraser (available at art supply stores).

When you have finished, you may want to redo the final step in India ink with a fine brush or pen. When the ink is dry, use the kneaded eraser to clean off the pencil lines. The eraser will not affect the India ink.

Here are some suggestions: In the first few steps, even

when all seems quite correct, you might do well to hold your work up to a mirror. Sometimes the mirror shows that you've twisted the drawing off to one side without being aware of it. At first you may find it difficult to draw the egg shapes, or ball shapes, or sausage shapes, or just to make the pencil go where you wish. Don't be discouraged. The more you practice, the more you will develop control. The only equipment you'll need will be a medium or soft pencil, paper, the kneaded eraser and, if you wish, a pen or brush and India ink.

The first steps in this book are shown darker than necessary so that they can be clearly seen. (Keep your work very light)

Remember there are many other ways and methods to make drawings. This book shows just one method. Why don't you seek out other ways from teachers, from libraries and, most importantly . . . from inside yourself?

Lee J. Ames

To the Parent or Teacher

"Leslie can draw a soccer player better than anybody else!" Such peer acclaim and encouragement generate incentive. Contemporary methods of art instruction (freedom of expression, experimentation, self-evaluation of competence and growth) provide a vigorous, fresh-air approach for which we must all be grateful.

New ideas need not, however, totally exclude the old. One such is the "follow me, step-by-step" approach. In my young learning days this method was so common, and frequently so exclusive, that the student became nothing more than a pantographic extension of the teacher. In those days it was excessively overworked.

This does not mean that the young hand is never to be guided. Rather, specific guiding is fundamental. Step-by-step guiding that produces satisfactory results is valuable even when the means of accomplishment are not fully understood by the student.

The novice with a musical instrument is frequently taught to play simple melodies as quickly as possible, well before he learns the most elemental scratchings at the surface of music theory. The resultant self-satisfaction, pride in accomplishment, can be a significant means of providing motivation. And all from mimicking an instructor's "Do-as-I-do. . . ."

Mimicry is prerequisite for developing creativity. We learn the use of our tools by mimicry. Then we can use those tools for creativity. To this end I would offer the budding artist the opportunity to memorize or mimic (rotelike, if you wish) the making of "pictures." "Pictures" he has been eager to be able to draw.

The use of this book should be available to anyone who *wants* to try another way of flapping his wings. Perhaps he will then get off the ground when his friend says, "Leslie can draw a soccer player better than anyone else!"

Lee J. Ames

Archery

Baseball—batting

Baseball—fielding

Baseball—pitching

Basketball—dribbling

Basketball—hook shot

Basketball—jump shot

Boxing—left hook

Boxing—right cross

Bowling

Diving—jacknife

Diving—swan

Fencing—en garde

Fencing—lunge

Football—linebacker

Football—running back

Golf

Gymnastics—balance beam

Gymnastics—pommel horse

Hockey—defense

Hockey—wing

Jai Alai (Pelota)—atchiki (momentary holding of the pelote)

Karate—back fist & sword foot

Karate—(middle level) front attack

Lacrosse

Racquetball—forehand

Sculling

Figure Skating

Skating—speed

Skiing—downhill

Ski Jump

Soccer—dribble

Soccer—head shot

Softball—pitcher

Surfing

Tennis—backhand

Tennis—forehand

Tennis—service

Track & Field—discus

Track & Field—distance

Track & Field—hammer throw

Track & Field—hurdles

Track & Field—javelin

Track & Field—shotput

Track & Field—sprinter

Volleyball—spike

Wrestling

(Continued)—Wrestling

Lee J. Ames has been earning his living as an artist for almost forty years. He began his career working on Walt Disney's *Fantasia* and *Pinocchio*. He has taught at the School of Visual Arts in Manhattan and, more recently, at Dowling College on Long Island. He was for a time director of his own advertising agency and illustrator for several magazines. Mr. Ames has illustrated over one hundred books, from preschool picture books to postgraduate texts. When not working, he battles on the tennis court. A native New Yorker, Lee J. Ames lives in Dix Hills, Long Island, with his wife, Jocelyn, their three dogs, and a calico cat.

DRAW 50 FOR HOURS OF FUN!

*Using Lee J. Ames's proven, step-by-step method of drawing instruction you can easily
learn to draw animals, monsters, airplanes, cars, sharks, buildings, dinosaurs, famous cartoons, and so much
more! Millions of people have learned to draw by using the award-winning
"Draw 50" technique. Now you can too!*

COLLECT THE ENTIRE DRAW 50 SERIES!

*The Draw 50 Series books are available from your local bookstore.
You may also order direct (make a copy of this form to order).*

Titles are paperback, unless otherwise indicated.

ISBN	TITLE	PRICE	QTY	TOTAL
23629-8	Airplanes, Aircraft, and Spacecraft	$8.95/$11.95 Can	X ____	= _____
19519-2	Animals	$8.95/$11.95 Can	X ____	= _____
24638-2	Athletes	$8.95/$11.95 Can	X ____	= _____
26767-3	Beasties and Yugglies and Turnover Uglies and Things That Go Bump in the Night	$8.95/$11.95 Can	X ____	= _____
23630-1	Boats, Ships, Trucks and Trains	$8.95/$11.95 Can	X ____	= _____
41777-2	Buildings and Other Structures	$8.95/$11.95 Can	X ____	= _____
24639-0	Cars, Trucks, and Motorcycles	$8.95/$11.95 Can	X ____	= _____
24640-4	Cats	$8.95/$11.95 Can	X ____	= _____
42449-3	Creepy Crawlies	$8.95/$11.95 Can	X ____	= _____
19520-6	Dinosaurs and Other Prehistoric Animals	$8.95/$11.95 Can	X ____	= _____
23431-7	Dogs	$8.95/$11.95 Can	X ____	= _____
46985-3	Endangered Animals	$8.95/$11.95 Can	X ____	= _____
19521-4	Famous Cartoons	$8.95/$11.95 Can	X ____	= _____
23432-5	Famous Faces	$8.95/$11.95 Can	X ____	= _____
47150-5	Flowers, Trees, and Other Plants	$8.95/$11.95 Can	X ____	= _____
26770-3	Holiday Decorations	$8.95/$11.95 Can	X ____	= _____
17642-2	Horses	$8.95/$11.95 Can	X ____	= _____
17639-2	Monsters	$8.95/$11.95 Can	X ____	= _____
41194-4	People	$8.95/$11.95 Can	X ____	= _____
47162-9	People of the Bible	$8.95/$11.95 Can	X ____	= _____
47005-3	People of the Bible (hardcover)	$13.95/$19.95 Can	X ____	= _____
26768-1	Sharks, Whales, and Other Sea Creatures	$8.95/$11.95 Can	X ____	= _____
14154-8	Vehicles	$8.95/$11.95 Can	X ____	= _____
	Shipping and handling	**(add $2.50 per order)**	X ____	= _____
		TOTAL		_____

Please send me the title(s) I have indicated above. I am enclosing $_____.
Send check or money order in U.S. funds only (no C.O.D.s or cash, please). Make check payable to
Doubleday Consumer Services. Allow 4 - 6 weeks for delivery.
Prices and availability are subject to change without notice.

Name:_____

Address:_____ Apt. # _____

City:_____ State:_____ ZIP Code: _____

Send completed coupon and payment to:
Doubleday Consumer Services
Dept. LA 7
2451 South Wolf Road
Des Plaines, IL 60018